GRACE FOR GLORY

JAMES A. RUSHTON

GRACE FOR GLORY
© 2009 By James A. Rushton

All rights reserved. No portion of this publication may be reproduced, stored in a retrieval system, or transmitted by any means—electronic, mechanical, photocopying, recording, or any other—except for brief quotations in printed reviews, without the prior written permission of the publisher.

Unless otherwise noted, all Scripture references are from the King James Translation of the Bible. Scripture references marked AMP are from the Amplified Bible, © 1954, 1958, 1962, 1964, 1965, 1987 by The Lockman Foundation. Scripture references marked MSG are from The Message © 1993, 1994, 1995, 1996, 2000, 2001, 2002 by Eugene H. Peterson. Scripture references marked NIV are from the New International Version, © 1973, 1978, 1984 by International Bible Society. Scripture references marked NKJV are from the New King James Version, © 1982 by Thomas Nelson, Inc. Scripture references marked NLT are from the New Living Translation, © 1996, 2004 by Tyndale Charitable Trust. Used by permission of Tyndale House Publishers.

Direct quotations from the Bible are in Italic type. Scripture passages in bold are made by the author for greater emphasis.

ISBN 978-0-9762744-1-4

Edited by:	Joshua D. Lease, Aegis Editing
	www.aegisediting.com
Layout by:	Charlene Panak, Image Design Plus
	Sand Springs, OK
Cover by:	Joy Hirschy, Word of Life Church
	Dubuque, IA
Printed by:	Lightning Source Inc

SPECIAL THANKS

Father thanks for loving us and making grace and glory.

Jesus thanks for paying the price for us to be able to receive this grace and glory.

Holy Spirit, thanks for revealing this grace and glory.

Mary thanks for being my most gracious and glorious wife. Thanks for being a most gracious and glorious mother to Jason. Mary thanks for being my lover, friend, and partner. Next to Jesus, you are the best thing that every came into my life.

Jason thanks for being teachable and allowing us to train you in the ways of the Lord. Your graciousness toward your mom and me is outstanding.

Pastor Loren and Joy thanks for being so gracious with your time and energy over the years as you listened and shared with me through many things. Thanks for your encouragement in the writing of this book. Joy, a special thanks to you for using one of your many talents in designing the cover of this book. Both of you are wonderful examples of God's love, grace, and glory.

Ruth thanks for your sincere, honest input as you read the manuscript. Thanks for your encouragement and thanks to you and John for being friends over the years

Pastor Joe and Barbara thanks for the both of you for being so gracious in receiving me as a minister of the Gospel. Thanks for your Christ-like talk and walk. Thanks to you also for encouraging me to do this book.

Pastor David and Becky thanks for being good, good to my family and me, and good examples of God's love and grace.

Joshua thanks you for using your intelligence, energy, and talent in editing. You sure have made me look good.

Charlene thanks for your wonderful way of laying out the book to make it easy to read.

Contents

Preface
vii

Chapter One
"Why This Title?"
9

Chapter Two
"Do Not Forget the "ing"
15

Chapter Three
"This Grace"
21

Chapter Four
"Warnings"
29

Chapter Five
"Grace and Truth"
47

Chapter Six
"Grace to Glory"
55

"Jesus is Lord, and He provides."

CHAPTER SEVEN
"JESUS WITH GRACE"
65

CHAPTER EIGHT
"GRACE IN THE BOOK OF ACTS"
73

CHAPTER NINE
"THREE KINDS OF GLORY"
83

CHAPTER TEN
"GRACE TO YOU FOR OTHERS"
95

ABOUT THE AUTHOR
105

PRAYER
106

"Jesus is Lord, and He provides."

Preface

I heard a speaker at a camp meeting say at the beginning of his message, "You do not need to know me to receive from God. But you do need to search the Scriptures to see if what I am saying is true."

So it is with me—you do not need to know me to receive what the Holy Spirit has taught me about His grace and glory. I urge you to search the Scriptures to see if what is shared in this book is true.

In my style of writing, I will bring some things to your attention that you will need to read more than once, because I desire to get you to think. Someone asked me whom this book was written for. I said, *"For the same people the Bible was written for—whosoever."*

It is my desire that you grow in God's grace and walk in His glory. As we allow these things to manifest in our lives, we can experience God's best and help others receive God's best for their lives.

As you read this book, allow this teaching to do to you what the Word of God desires to do in your life. My job description is to help this happen with the help of the Holy Spirit, as I stand in the office of a teacher. This job description is in *Ephesians 4:12-16:*

> *And for the equipping of the saints for the work of ministry, for the edifying of the body of Christ, till we all come to the unity of the faith and of the*

knowledge of the Son of God, to a perfect man, to the measure of the stature of the fullness of Christ; that we should no longer be children, tossed to and fro and carried about with every wind of doctrine, by the trickery of men, in the cunning craftiness of deceitful plotting, but, speaking the truth in love, may grow up in all things into Him who is the head — Christ — from whom the whole body, joined and knit together by what every joint supplies, according to the effective working by which every part does its share, causes growth of the body for the edifying of itself in love.

It is my prayer that we all become better equipped and full of grace and truth to bring about the manifestation of God's glory, which is in us by Christ Jesus.

If this is what you desire, read on and allow the Holy Spirit to minister this teaching to you.

Chapter One

"Why This Title?"

As the title says, this book is about grace for glory, so why not just call it *Grace* or just call it *Glory*? This is because one cannot experience grace with out glory. Any time you see the true grace of God in operation, you will also see God's glory revealed. In addition, any time you see God's glory, you will see either God directly or man allowing His grace to bring about His glory.

I became interested in grace and glory about three years ago, even though I wish it had been sooner. In my former years, I was all about faith, healing, the Holy Ghost, and doing the works of Jesus. These are still high on my list, but I needed to expand my list of thinking and operation.

I became concerned that I was not seeing the grace and glory of God that we read about in both the Old Testament and New Testament. So I began to pray and study these things.

The primary Scriptures that the Holy Spirit brought to my attention to see how grace and glory work together are in Exodus. We will look more closely at these chapters later on in this book, but let me point out that Moses saw the grace and glory of God inside as well as outside of the tabernacle. Moses started talking about the grace of God, which led him to ask God to show him His glory, and God did.

Exodus 33:12-17 says,

Then Moses said to the LORD, "See, You say to me, 'Bring up this people.' But You have not let me know whom You will send with me. Yet You have said,' I know you by name, and you have also found grace in My sight.' Now therefore, I pray, if I have found grace in Your sight, show me now Your way, that I may know You and that I may find grace in Your sight. And consider that this nation is Your people." And He said," My Presence will go with you, and I will give you rest." Then he said to Him," If Your Presence does not go with us, do not bring us up from here. For how then will it be known that Your people and I have found grace in Your sight, except You go with us? So we shall be separate, Your people and I, from all the people who are upon the face of the earth." So the LORD said to Moses," I will also do this thing that you have spoken; for you have found grace in My sight, and I know you by name" (NKJV).

Moses continues to talk to God in verse eighteen saying, *"Please show me Your glory."* God tells Moses, *"I will."* Then God allows His goodness to pass before Moses. However, that was not all: the Lord God and Moses continue talking and in *Exodus 34:1-4*, God tells Moses to cut two tablets like the first ones. Then God said, *"I will write on them the same thing I did on the first ones."*

Is that not wonderful? God does not change, and He is the God of second chances.

Then after all of this, the Lord continued to show Moses His glory.

> *Exodus 34:6 (NKJV)*
> *And the LORD passed before him and proclaimed, "The LORD, the LORD God, merciful and gracious, longsuffering, and abounding in goodness and truth...*

> *After hearing of God's grace and seeing God's glory, Moses said in verse nine, "If now I have found grace in thy sight, O LORD, let my LORD, I pray thee, go among us; for it is a stiffnecked people; and pardon our iniquity and our sin, and take us for thine inheritance" (Exodus 34:9).*

But the truth is Moses had found grace in the sight of God. Look at verse ten, in which God said, *"Behold, I make a covenant. Before all your people I will do marvels such as have not been done in all the earth, nor in any nation; and all the people among whom you are shall see the work of the LORD. For it is an awesome thing that I will do with you"* (NKJV).

In other words, God said, *"Yes, you have found grace, and I will go with you."* Is that not what happens to us who have called on the Lord to be saved? We find grace that saves us through faith. It is wonderful what faith will make available to us when we put it into practice. When we talk, walk, and stand in faith, it shows us in a tangible way God's grace, which saves us, and God by His Spirit has been with us ever since.

Ephesians 2:8 (NKJV)
For by grace you have been saved through faith, and that not of yourselves; it is the gift of God...

The founder of Rhema Bible Training Center, Kenneth E. Hagin, once said, "Studying faith is like looking at a mountain. You can look at a mountain from many sides and get a different view, but it is the same mountain." Grace is like that. Grace has many varieties or many sides, but it is still grace.

What is grace? Grace is God's divine influence acting in man, bringing forth favorable results. Grace works to bring God's purposes to manifestation through the willing response of men to His grace. Grace also brings us into a new power alignment.

You will see the definitions more clearly as we look into God's Word regarding grace.

There are two other words in the title—*"for"* and *"glory."* Receiving grace in order to be saved and walking in grace is about bringing glory to the Father and to His son Jesus. The purpose or aim of grace is to bring forth our salvation *"for"* God's glory. Friend, you and I are the specific people for whom God designed grace. Grace is also to be used in a specific way that is to bring glory to God.

Now, let us look at the word *"glory."* Glory has many different definitions. Just like grace, you can look at it from many sides, as a mountain, and see a different view but it is the same mountain.

Glory means to boast, to have joy, to rejoice in, to be heavy or weighty, to be honored and to be great. Glory also means to have a good opinion of God's attributes, ways, and power. In addition to all these definitions, glory also means to give honor.

Let us keep these definitions in our hearts as we continue to learn about His grace for His glory.

> **Grace is aimed to you, to bring forth His glory.**

Chapter Two

"Do Not Forget the "ing"?

The name I wanted to give this book in the beginning was *"Grace for Gracing and Gracing for Grace."*

The first time I heard the word *"gracing"* was when it came out of my mouth while I was studying and praying about grace. After I said it, I was not sure I wanted to look up the word in the dictionary because I was not sure it was in there. Guess what—it wasn't (at least not in the way I meant it). But I did look up the meaning of the verb tense *"ing,"* and this adjusted my thinking about words such as love, forgiveness, give, faith, grace, and many other words throughout God's Word.

According to Webster's New World Dictionary, adding *"ing"* to a word causes it to mean action or process, to be the product or result of an action or process, or to be something connected with, consisting of, or used in making of a specified thing.

Based on the definitions above, let's list some words we should have an "ing" attached to. Love becomes loving, give to giving, forgive to forgiving, testify to testifying, worship to worshipping, praise to praising, pray to praying, revive to reviving, and faith to faithing, and grace to gracing.

These words are some that apply to our Christian walk. For you to better understand, let me give you this example. If someone has a boat and the boat is at the dock, it is just a boat. But when someone takes the boat on the water and travels over the water, we can say he or she is "boating."

Well, the things of God must be taken out of dock and put into operation. With the boat, the owner determines when, where, and why the boat should be at the dock. The owner also decides when, where, and why the boat should be put into operation. We need a place to dock in our lives—and we have one.

Let's still use the boat example. In the life of a boat, there are two docks available for the boat. One dock is called dry dock. This is where the owner docks it for repair, restoration, and major cleaning. The other dock is a dock where the boat is just sitting in the water, waiting on someone to take it out boating. At both docks there is protection.

There are three areas in which we can put ourselves into God's *"docks."* The first is in the area of our own personal time of prayer and studying of God's Word. The second is in the local church, which preaches, teaches, and practices the things of God. Third is spending time having fellowship with people of like faith. Each of these places were designed by God for us to be repaired, restored, cleaned, and protected for the Master's use.

I could say much more about comparing the care and operation of a boat to the care and operation of our lives, but let me take time to say this. Two of the many things that are done to a boat to protect it and help it last a long time are when the owner washes it down regularly with soap and water and when he paints it with an anti-fouling paint.

Similarly, we are to be separated and washed with the washing of the Word. *Ephesians 5:26-27* says He does this for His bride, *"That He might sanctify and cleanse her with the washing of water by the word, that He might present her to Himself a glorious church, not having spot or wrinkle or any such thing, but that she should be holy and without blemish."*

We are to be washed by the blood also. When we are walking in the light and having fellowship with one another, the blood cleanses us. General Electric was not the first with a self-cleaning system when they put them in their ovens. God had a self-cleaning system available long ago. It is called fellowship.

> *1 John 1:7 (NKJV)*
> *But if we walk in the light as He is in the light, we have fellowship with one another, and the blood of Jesus Christ His Son cleanses us from all sin.*

Notice what *Hebrews 12:4* tells us: *"Ye have not yet resisted unto blood, striving against sin." (KJV)* The blood is the soap of the Gospel. One can take a bath every day for a week with just water and at the end of the week still smell bad. But if one uses soap and water daily, one will not smell bad—you will be clean.

The washing of the water by the Word clears up our thinking as we get our minds renewed with the Word of God. It gets rid of stinking thinking, which if not cleared out, will lead to sin. Yes, we do have 1 *John 1:9*, which says, *"If we confess our sins, He is faithful and just to forgive us our sins and to cleanse us from all unrighteousness."*

We have the Word, Spirit, and the blood to help us keep our boat—our lives—in tiptop shape. We have the same three things the angels of heaven had in *Revelation 12:7-12*—they had the testimony of the Word of God, the Spirit, and the blood. Contrast this with what *1 John 5:8* says: *"And there are three that bear witness on earth: the Spirit, the water, and the blood; and these three agree as one."*

With the boat the owner applies soap and water and the anti-fouling paint to his boat. With us, we use the

Spirit and apply the water (the Word) and the blood to our lives.

When we do, the following things will take place: One, the Spirit will lead us to truth. Two, the Word will clear up our thinking. Three, the blood will wash away every weight, mark, and smear of sin. This regular maintenance keeps us in tip-top shape, ever ready for the Master's use, as we stay "docked" in the right place.

So as we continue our walk, let's remember to add the *"ing."*

> **Grace is the seed of glory**
> **Grace is the glory begun.**

Chapter Three

"This Grace"

What is this grace? How did we get it? How do we grow in grace?

What is grace?

Grace is God's divine influence acting in man, bringing forth favorable results. Grace works to bring God's purposes to manifestation through the willing response of men to His grace. Grace also brings us into a new power alignment.

This new power alignment took place when you were saved by grace through faith. Your faith, the faith that God gave you, is what flips the switch for grace to go into operation. This was put in place to deliver you from the power of darkness into the power of His dear Son, which is the kingdom of light.

> *Colossians 1:13 says, "He has delivered us from the power of darkness and conveyed us into the kingdom of the Son of His love" (NKJV).*

Before Christ was in our lives, we had no lasting power. Yes, we had some power in the flesh, and we had some power from the kingdom of darkness. But neither one of these will last forever. Now with Christ in our lives, we have available the power of the Kingdom of God and all it stands for—forever. We have a new power of not just the name of Jesus, not just the Word of God, not just the power of the Holy Ghost, but a power called *"grace."* We also have the power of love, the power of faith, the power of forgiveness, the power to give, and much more because of grace bringing us into this new power alignment, connected with the Kingdom of God.

As a result of this new power alignment, you are now in a position to receive more of God's favor.

How do we get this grace?

Most people reading this book know they were saved by grace. But let's look at some Scriptures to help us see it more clearly. These and the rest of this book will help you see you received more than you expected and that more is expected of us in relationship to grace.

One thing you should see is that you receive much more grace than you could imagine. You receive a grace to help you stand and reign in life, so you can serve the Lord by serving others.

> *John 1:16-17 (NKJV)*
> *And of His fullness we have all received, and grace for grace. For the law was given through Moses, but grace and truth came through Jesus Christ.*

In the beginning of your Christian life, you got grace by faith, because you made a decision to believe on the Lord Jesus Christ and to confess this belief with your mouth. This was based on *Romans 10:8-10*, which says,

> *But what does it say? 'The word is near you, in your mouth and in your heart' (that is, the word of faith which we preach): that if you confess with your mouth the Lord Jesus and believe in your heart that God has raised Him from the dead, you will be saved. For with the heart one believes unto righteousness, and with the mouth confession is made unto salvation.*

Let's look at the following verses, which will help us understand that God did not just design grace for us to be born again. He designed it as one of those things we are to use to reign in life through Jesus Christ.

> *Romans 5:17 (NIV)*
> *For if, by the trespass of the one man, death reigned through that one man, how much more will those who receive God's abundant provision of grace and of the gift of righteousness reign in life through the one man, Jesus Christ.*

Yes, grace is first used to help us receive freedom from sin and cause us to receive what we did not deserve. But please understand we are to go from that point to reigning in life by grace and the gift of righteousness.

I'll bring something else to your attention that will help you by saying grace is a teacher and this teacher will help you live a righteous, holy life, free from sin. This is what *Titus 2:11-12* tells us. *"For the grace of God that brings salvation has appeared to all men, teaching us that, denying ungodliness and worldly lusts, we should live soberly, righteously, and godly in the present age."*

This verse is from the New King James Version. The section has a heading at the beginning that says, *"Training by Saving Grace."* Praise the Lord, grace is a teacher, and it will train you to deny ungodliness and worldly lust. This is very important because when we are right with God and living right, God's grace is manifested and His glory is seen.

Do not get the opinion that I am saying grace is replacing the work of the Holy Spirit. I am not.

Remember what Jesus said about the Holy Spirit? He said He would teach us, guide us, and lead us. There are many things the Holy Spirit will teach, lead, and guide us to, and one of these is grace. The Holy Spirit will introduce us to Jesus, to love, to faith, to forgiveness, and to grace—plus much more, including to Himself.

After the Holy Spirit has introduced you to these elements of God's Kingdom, these things will start speaking. Love has a voice, faith has a voice, forgiveness has a voice, prosperity has a voice, and grace has a voice.

When these voices speak, they train us on how to walk in what that voice represents.

Hebrews 10:29 mentions *"the Spirit of Grace."* Just like love and faith, which are spirits and are attributes of the heart of the Father, grace is a spirit and one of those attributes.

Just think about it—both God's Kingdom and the devil's are spiritual kingdoms, and both operate on the same principles. The devil's kingdom has spirits of hate, fear, unbelief, bitterness, lying, and many others, and they are all attributes of the devil. The spirit of hate teaches people to hate. The spirits of devilish ways teach people to act certain ways of the devil. The devil has demonic teachers so they can try to influence us to their ways and characteristics, causing us to be like one of them. They do this by using words, and these words identify who and what they are.

It reminds me of a school system where they have the superintendent, the principal, the teachers, and students. Note one superintendent, one principal, but many teachers and many students. The principal hires the teachers, giving each a subject to teach.

Well, look at the Holy Spirit as a principal who assigns teachers in the spirit realm to teach us. There is a teacher of love, a teacher of faith, a teacher of forgiveness, a teacher of prosperity, and a teacher called grace. Yes, God has teachers in the Body of Christ who teach us what the spiritual teachers have taught them. This is what I am doing with this book—teaching you what grace taught me about grace.

Grace has taught me what frustrates it. Grace has taught me how to stand in grace. Grace has taught me about how to release this grace to others, and I am still learning of this grace. Grace has taught me how to obtain mercy to find grace to help in a time of need.

Expand your subjects, and as you do, your operation in the Spirit will greatly improve and bring more glory to Him.

So how do we grow in grace?

2 Peter 3:18 (NKJV)
But grow in the grace and knowledge of our Lord and Savior Jesus Christ. To Him be the glory both now and forever. Amen.

The growth process was put into motion the day you received Jesus as your personal Lord and Savior. I do not know you, but ask yourself this question: What things of God have you grown in since you were saved? I believe there have been some things, and by the fact you are reading this book, you must have a desire to grow in grace for His glory.

Suppose your answer to the question was that you've grown in faith. To grow in faith, you probably purchased all the recordings and books you could and studied them as you prayed and thought about faith. You grew in faith because you set your heart and mind to learn about faith, having your mind renewed with the Word of God on the subject of faith. Then you exercised that faith, causing it to develop.

To continue to increase in grace and grow, you must make a decision to learn of grace. Remember, just like learning something in the natural, it costs of your time and finances to learn. But it pays! In the Kingdom of God, it costs of your time and finances, but it pays as you learn and will continue to pay as long as you apply the knowledge you have of the subject.

Apples produce apples. Dogs produce dogs. People produce people. Things produce after their own kind—not only in the natural but also in the spirit. Grace produces grace. Love produces love. Faith produces faith. On the negative side, hate produces hate. Fear produces fear. Bitterness produces bitterness.

Remember nothing can produce in a vacuum. Living things need something to activate reproduction. Sure, there are other things involved for the fruit to come forth; but simply stated, the woman needs a seed from a man. An apple tree needs the pollen from the bloom of another tree.

So what does grace need so it can produce? It needs faith. Whether it is the woman, the apple tree, or grace, the giver of life in all three is God the Father. Yet, as with all His creation, He designs all of it to need something else. He created it to produce. It is the heart of God that nothing be alone, so His creation cannot reproduce when it has its missing component.

I want to go back to the new birth experience to illustrate how faith and grace come to manifest in one's life. There was something very important on the scene when you used faith to activate the grace of God to become His child. That something was love. On God's part, love was flowing all the time, and when you showed your love to Him and planted the seed to become His child, a supernatural thing took place by the power of the Holy Spirit at a very supernatural speed.

The Holy Spirit is so great; He introduces us to the Word. Then He stands by to watch over that Word to perform it as you use faith to activate that Word. When you do, He causes that Word to produce. The Word of God will produce on any subject as you hear, believe, receive, and act out that subject.

> **Grace is the seed of glory**
> **Grace is glory begun**
> **Glory is grace perfected**
> **Grace will produce glory.**

Chapter Four

"Warnings"

I noticed many years ago that for every promise or provision in the Word of God, there is always something we were to do or not do in order to see the promise come to pass. There are conditions that must be met for us to operate in and receive the things of God. Most of the time, we like to focus on the good things we are to do to cause God's kind of things to happen.

For example, we like to stand on the promise that if we give it will be given back to us, but there are some conditions to this promise. We are to give what the Word and Holy Spirit tells us. The Word tells us to give of our tithes and offerings. The Holy Spirit will tell you who and how to give, but the Word tells us to give our tithes—and tithes means ten percent. Another condition to this promise is to give cheerfully and to do it in love and faith.

So when it comes to grace, what are the conditions for us keeping ourselves in this grace not only for it to bless us but also for it to flow through us to help others?

In the book of Hebrews and the book of Galatians, we see some warnings pertaining to staying in this grace.

There are four warnings I need to bring to our attention. If we take heed to these and see that we may be operating under one of these warnings, we can make changes and allow grace to flow.

Warning #1—Do not come up short.

Hebrews 12:15 (NIV)
See to it that no one misses the grace of God and that no bitter root grows up to cause trouble and defile many.

This verse tells us not to fall short of the grace of God. Well, how can you tell if you have come up short of the grace of God? If any root of bitterness is there, you are coming up short. When one is bitter, there is no graciousness, thereby hindering grace. Bitterness brings defilement to you and many others. Bitterness is a spirit, and spirits penetrate.

Look at how the Message Bible translates this verse: *"Make sure no one gets left out of God's generosity. Keep a sharp eye out for weeds of bitter discontent. A thistle or two gone to seed can ruin a whole garden in no time."*

How does one get to a point where they are walking in bitterness? One way is by not walking in generosity towards people.

I had to deal with something like this very recently in my life. Something took place beyond my control regarding some outreach work that caused some tension between another person and me. Even though no one knew about it but the two of us, we began to be less friendly towards one another. I became a little bitter towards this person, and I begin to back off in wanting to do anything with the person.

This only lasted about one month, and that was one month too long. I mean, I was in the middle of writing this book on grace and being gracious, and here I was not being careful and slipped right into bitterness, causing me to come up short of the grace of God. I left this person out of the generosity of God. When I left this person out, it left me out, and it was affecting God's garden.

Well, I guess you may be wondering how this grace became active in our lives again. We ended up in a working situation where we were working within two feet of each other helping some other people. These other people were not church people. We were working as a team helping these people who were down and out. We were ministering together, with both of us showing much love, grace, and kindness towards these other people.

And the Holy Spirit spoke to me. He asked me, "Why are you so loving, gracious, and kind to these people, but yet you have this attitude towards this co-worker who has done no wrong?"

After hearing this, all I could say was, "Forgive me." And I started praying in the Holy Ghost to myself, then turned to this person and said, "Thank you for helping. I love you." Then we gave each other a big hug, and all has been well since.

Regardless of how spiritual we may think we are, we must always be careful, making sure we are walking in grace and having no bitterness by being gracious towards all people.

Warning #2—Do not turn to another gospel.

> *Galatians 1:6 (NKJV)*
> *I marvel that you are turning away so soon from Him who called you in the grace of Christ, to a different gospel.*

Being led to believe anything other than the Gospel of Jesus Christ will stop the grace of God in your life. Following are three translations that may help you understand this with their different ways of explaining it.

> *Hebrews 13:9 (NLT)*
> *So do not be attracted by strange, new ideas. Your spiritual strength comes from God's special favor,*

not from ceremonial rules about food, which don't help those who follow them.

Hebrews 13:9 (NIV)
Do not be carried away by all kinds of strange teachings. It is good for our hearts to be strengthened by grace, not by ceremonial foods, which are of no value to those who eat them.

Hebrews 13:9 (MSG)
Don't be lured away from him by the latest speculations about him. The grace of Christ is the only good ground for life. Products named after Christ don't seem to do much for those who buy them.

In *John 1:17* we read that grace and truth came through Jesus Christ. *John 14:6* tells us, "Jesus said, *'I am the way, the truth, and the life. No one comes to the Father except through Me."*

So in *Galatians 1:6*, Paul says, *"I marvel that you are so soon removed from him that called you into the grace of Christ unto another Gospel."*

This word *"gospel"* is a very important word that we need to know the complete meaning of. To Christians, the Gospel is the teachings of Jesus Christ and the Apostles, which is recorded in the Holy Bible. But this is not the complete definition of the word gospel. A gospel is a belief or body of beliefs proclaimed or accepted as absolutely true. We would call other gospels false religions, but to the people who teach and believe them, they are the gospel.

The Gospel of the Lord Jesus Christ is not the only gospel out there for people to hear, believe, and receive. That is why you need to judge all teachings against the true Gospel of the Lord Jesus Christ. Do what they did in *Acts 17:11*, which says, *"These were more fair-minded than those in Thessalonica, in that they received the word with all readiness, and searched the Scriptures daily to find out whether these things were so" (NKJV).*

If you read the Book of Jude, you will see the book is written to warn of false teachers or other gospels in which many were being led astray. Most people who have received Jesus as their Lord and Savior came from another gospel that gave them no freedom. So this makes it very important that you compare all you hear with the Gospel of the Lord Jesus Christ, which is the truth.

The Book of Jude not only warns us of false teachers of other gospels, it also shows us very clearly one of several things of importance that we can do to keep us free from other gospels that are not true. *"But you, beloved, building yourselves up on your most holy faith, praying in the Holy Spirit, keep yourselves in the love of God, looking for the mercy of our Lord Jesus Christ unto eternal life" (Jude 20-21 NKJV).*

Notice this verse says we are to be building ourselves up in our most holy faith. Remember, the book of Jude is about us staying hooked up with the Gospel of the Lord Jesus Christ.

I like to say it this way—*"praying in the Holy Ghost helps us stay in the faith of Christianity by keeping us in the love of God"*. There is a lot of difference between staying in faith for a new pair of shoes versus staying in the faith of Christianity.

What is the difference? When you just stay in faith for things, you will be an open target for other gospels. Why? Because you can easily get sidetracked with the things of life instead of a lifestyle of Christianity (by His Word and the help of the Holy Ghost). This is why many Christians are led into another gospel.

There are a number of things we can do to guard ourselves and to keep from falling into another gospel. Let me list a few:

1. Hear the Word of God.
2. Believe the Word of God.
3. Do the Word of God.
4. Study the Word of God.
5. Get involved with a Word Church.
6. Have fellowship with those of like precious faith.
7. Love the Lord your God with all your passion, prayers, intelligence, energy, and muscle.
8. Give of your tithes and offerings.
9. Praise Him.
10. Worship Him.
11. Pray, pray, pray.

Those who have gone the way of another gospel or the way of sin were led that way because of failing to do these things.

We must be sure we are following the gospel of the Lord Jesus Christ.

Warning #3—Do not frustrate the grace of God

Let's look at two Scriptures about grace that perhaps you have not given much attention. The Apostle Paul wrote them both. Paul was one of the many writers in the New Testament that asked that grace and peace be multiplied to us and that we should grow in grace. Paul is also the one Jesus spoke to and said, *"My grace is sufficient for you" (2 Corinthians 12:9).*

Most everything Paul said about grace was on the positive side, yet at times he gave us written warnings to keep us out of the negative. That is why he told us we should not *"frustrate"* the grace of God and we should not be one of those who had brought *"despite"* to the grace of God.

In *Galatians 2:21*, Paul says, *"I do not frustrate the grace of God: for if righteousness comes by the law, then Christ is dead in vain" (KJV).* The author of Hebrews says, *"...and hath done despite unto the Spirit of grace?" (Hebrews 10:29 KJV)*

Take a look at *Galatians 2:21* in two other translations: *"I do not set aside the grace of God; for if righteousness comes through the law, then Christ died in vain" (NIV).* *"[Therefore, I do not treat God's gracious gift as something of minor importance and defeat its very purpose]; I do not set aside and invalidate and frustrate and nullify the grace (unmerited favor) of God..." (AMP)*

Let's look at this using the word *"frustrate"* as the King James Version does. *"Frustrate"* means to make ineffectual, to bring to nothing, to make invalid, to make of no effect. It implies making vain or ineffectual all efforts, however vigorous or persistent.

Doing things our own way without the leadership of the Holy Spirit will frustrate the grace of God, causing the plan of God not to be done. This also grieves or quenches the Spirit. Grieving or quenching the Holy Spirit affects grace. This could cause you not to be blessed or cause someone else not to be blessed.

We could also frustrate the grace of God even though we are doing what God said because we are not doing it graciously. One can speak the truth of God's Word, but if it is not spoken graciously, it will have no positive effect.

Jesus was the most powerful person to ever walk on this earth. What was it about Jesus that drew people to Him? Was it because He walked around with a halo around His head? No. Was it because He walked around with this golden robe on? No. Remember what Jesus claimed His ministry was in *Luke 4:18-19:*

The Spirit of the LORD is upon Me, because He has anointed Me to preach the gospel to the poor; He has sent Me to heal the brokenhearted, to proclaim liberty to the captives and recovery of sight to the blind, to set at liberty those who are oppressed; to proclaim the acceptable year of the LORD. (NKJV)

After He had spoken these powerful words, this is how the people responded: *"So all bore witness to Him, and marveled at the gracious words which proceeded out of His mouth…" (Luke 4:22 NKJV)* They marveled at how graciously He spoke.

Some people are like I used to be. They think if it is not loud, it has no power or authority. But that is not true.

Note what else the people said about Jesus in *Matthew 7:28-29: "The people were astonished at His teaching, for He taught them as one who had authority."*

Believers who speak graciously will draw people, and they will teach with authority. In my early years and part of my middle years in the ministry, I taught and preached the truth of God's Word with power and authority, with great things happening, because God was honoring His Word and the faith of the people who heard that Word. But I do not remember anyone telling me I preached graciously.

Then one day when I had finished preaching in a friend's church in Tulsa, OK, we went out to dinner, and this is what he said to me: "James, you preach the truth, but you need to mix grace and mercy with that truth."

You see, my problem before was that I had declared war on the devil and anything he stood for and would preach him out, but I tended to forget the people. Jesus did both. He spoke graciously and with authority, casting out devils and healing all manner of sickness and disease among the people. Jesus was against the devil, but He was for people. One of the things that helped me was when I learned I was to preach and teach for people—not to them. Many young people are kept away because of parents and others speaking to them all the time and not speaking for them. Jesus came to earth for man.

It is easy for most people to speak graciously in church and around their pastor, and that is good, but we need to learn to speak graciously at home and in the market place. Why is this important? Because we need to live a life so people will receive us. Why? For the gospel's sake and their sake. Jesus said, *"He who receives you receives Me, and he who receives Me receives Him who sent Me."* (Matthew 10:40 NKJV)

Yes, we are to walk in love; but one of the things we need to do to walk in love is to be gracious—not just with the giving of things but also with our mouths.

We need to avoid frustrating or making the grace of God ineffective.

Warning #4—Do not do despite, or insult, grace.

The word despite is used in the King James Version of the Bible. *"Despite"* means to disrespect, to provoke, or to check or defeat another's plan or block the achievement of a goal.

God's grace was sent for a purpose, and anything man does to cause it not to be received by the target brings despite to God's grace.

> *Hebrews 10:29*
> *Of how much sorer punishment, suppose ye, shall he be thought worthy, who hath trodden under foot the Son of God, and hath counted the blood of the covenant, wherewith he was sanctified, an unholy thing, and hath done despite unto the Spirit of grace?*

The New King James Version uses the word *"insult."*

> *Hebrews 10:29 (NKJV)*
> *Of how much worse punishment, do you suppose, will he be thought worthy who has trampled the*

Son of God underfoot, counted the blood of the covenant by which he was sanctified a common thing, and insulted the Spirit of grace?

Many people have gone their own way and insulted the Spirit and grace of God for their lives simply because they would not do what God said. Others have gone their own way and have insulted the Spirit of grace for themselves, because after they heard it spoken in love and grace, they did not receive what was said.

I *"did despite"* to the Spirit of grace the first time someone shared Jesus with me. I just rebelled against it and insulted (or did despite) to the Spirit of grace for over fifteen years.

But, Praise the Lord, we have a God who is full of mercy and always has His grace available to save us the very second we use our faith to activate it. The faith and grace to be saved was there all the time, and it could reach us wherever we may have been at any time. All we needed to do was stop insulting this grace. No one likes to be insulted—not you, not I, not your loved ones, certainly not God, not Jesus and His Word, not the Holy Spirit, and not grace.

Think about the many people who have spent much of their Christian lives frustrating the grace of God or bringing insult to His grace. Now that you are thinking about them, stop and pray. Pray the spirit of grace is not just released upon them but that the eyes of their understanding are opened to this grace and their ears hear what the spirit of grace is saying. Pray the Lord of Harvest sends forth-gracious laborers to them.

I may as well say this while I am on the subject of frustrating and bringing despite to the grace of God. Let's look at what is said in 2 Corinthians 8:7 and 9.

2 Corinthians 8:7;9 (NKJV)
But as you abound in everything—in faith, in speech, in knowledge, in all diligence, and in your love for us—see that you abound in this grace also… For you know the grace of our Lord Jesus Christ, that though He was rich, yet for your sakes He became poor, that you through His poverty might become rich.

There are many things listed here we are to abound in, and one of them is *"grace."* What grace? The one talked about in verse nine. Yet many people have frustrated grace and caused despite to this grace to be made rich. They have done this by depending on foreign aid instead of Kingdom aid.

How do you think this grace feels knowing you need finances and instead you purchase a lottery ticket?

How do you think this grace feels that every time you need something you go to man and not your heavenly Father? I'll tell you how it feels. It feels insulted, and I can imagine faith feels the same way.

What do you think grace can do when you do not give of your tithes and offerings the way God's Word teaches? Nothing. What would you do if the next time you frustrated or insulted grace that grace would just say, "What you are doing is frustrating me. Would you please stop? If you do, I will help you."

Some people have only made grace happy in their lives once, and that was when they were first born again and were saved by it. Since that time, many are just living under mercy. Mercy is great, because if it were not for mercy, most of us would be dead! But just because we are under mercy does not mean we are receiving God's best. Yes, we can find mercy in the throne room of grace, but to receive God's best, we must let grace help. Mercy will keep you until you go to grace, but it takes faith. This is one of the main reasons we are commanded to live by faith—so we can activate grace.

Habakkuk 2:4
But the just shall live by his faith.

Romans 1:17
For therein is the righteousness of God revealed from faith to faith: as it is written, The just shall live by faith.

Galatians 3:11
But that no man is justified by the law in the sight of God, it is evident: for, The just shall live by faith.

Hebrews 10:38
Now the just shall live by faith: but if any man draw back, my soul shall have no pleasure in him.

Hebrews 11:6
But without faith it is impossible to please him: for he that cometh to God must believe that he is, and that he is a rewarder of them that diligently seek him.

There are many reasons why living by faith pleases the Father. First, it proves we have our heart on Him. Another reason is that it activates the grace of God in our lives, which causes things to happen for us and through us to bring forth the glory of God.

Walking in the love of God and living by faith will keep us in the Gospel of truth. Walking in the love of God and living by faith will keep us from coming up short. Walking in the love of God and living by faith will keep us from frustrating the grace of God and certainly keep us from bringing despite or insulting grace.

This is why the first commandment is number one—love the Lord your God with all your passion, with all your prayers, with all your intelligence, and all your energy.

Notice the word your, not someone else's passion, not someone else's prayers, not someone else's' intelligence, and not someone else's energy. Yours.

Mark 12:29-30 (MSG)
Jesus said, "The first in importance is, 'Listen, Israel: The Lord your God is one; so love the Lord God with all your passion and prayer and intelligence and energy."

> **Activate your faith to release God's grace to you, for you, and through you.**

Chapter Five

"Grace and Truth"

> *John 1:14 (NKJV)*
> *And the Word became flesh and dwelt among us, and we beheld His glory, the glory as of the only begotten of the Father, full of grace and truth.*

The Word, Jesus, came to walk on this earth before men in grace and truth, for all to see the glorious Father. Jesus did not stop by just coming in grace and truth. He also operated in glory and gave of this grace and truth. If we would read all the signs, wonders, miracles, and healings Jesus performed while on earth, we would easily see it was God's grace flowing through Him. He was here to show forth God's grace and glory in their lives.

The very first miracle Jesus performed with the help of the disciples was when He turned the water into wine at the wedding in Cana in *John 2:1-11*. Verse eleven says *He did it to manifest His glory*. Why? So the disciples would believe in Him. Yet it took an act of grace to bring it forth.

Jesus turning the water into wine was nothing but an act of graciousness to help a newlywed couple. Jesus did not stop with just walking in grace and truth. He also gave us of this grace and truth.

John 1:16 (NKJV)
And of His fullness we have all received, and grace for grace.

John 1:16 (AMP)
For out of His fullness (abundance) we have all received [all had a share and we were all supplied with] one grace after another and spiritual blessing upon spiritual blessing and even favor upon favor and gift [heaped] upon gift.

This lines up with the following Scripture:

2 Peter 1:3-4 (NKJV)
As His divine power has given to us all things that pertain to life and godliness, through the knowledge of Him who called us by glory and virtue, by which have been given to us exceedingly great and precious promises, that through these you may be partakers of the divine nature, having escaped the corruption that is in the world through lust.

If we want others to see Jesus in us, we need to walk in the same grace and truth Jesus did. He gave it to us so we could walk in grace and truth so others would see it and be blessed. When we do not walk in God's grace and truth, we frustrate the grace of God for others and ourselves.

Notice Jesus also came in truth. There are many truths in God's Word, and we should know them, because knowing and walking in these truths makes us free. Let me give you some examples of this. The truth is that the just are to live by faith. That is a truth. If we do not live by faith, we are not walking in our side of truth. The truth is that we are not to frustrate grace. If we do, we are not living in that truth. The truth is that by His stripes we were healed. If we do not believe and walk in that truth, we are not doing our side of that truth. The same principle applies to love, forgiveness, grace, and many other concepts in God's Word.

Grace and truth are very important to our lives—not just the God side but also our side. We are to walk in grace and truth the same as Jesus did under the direction of the Holy Spirit. Graciousness must be based on the Word of God in order to bring forth God's glory. There are people who are not born again who are very gracious simply because they desire to be or have been trained to be gracious. I know people like this, and yet they do not see signs and wonders and things that show forth God's glory. Why? Because their graciousness is based on human conduct apart from the Word of truth.

For graciousness to produce God's glory it must be based on God's Word under the direction of the Holy

Spirit; anything else brings glory to man and self and not to God.

Note what the following Scripture says:

Acts 20:32 (NKJV)
"So now, brethren, I commend you to God and to the word of His grace, which is able to build you up and give you an inheritance among all those who are sanctified.

Acts 20:32 (AMP)
And now [brethren], I commit you to God [I deposit you in His charge, entrusting you to His protection and care]. And I commend you to the Word of His grace [to the commands and counsels and promises of His unmerited favor]. It is able to build you up and to give you [your rightful] inheritance among all God's set-apart ones (those consecrated, purified, and transformed of soul).

Luke wrote the book of Acts, and he was a close traveling companion of Paul. Here in Acts, Luke is telling us what Paul said. Paul first committed the people to God and then to the Word of His grace, because he knew that putting God first was most important and that this must be done by God's Word. Paul knew the grace of the Lord Jesus Christ would be sufficient if God's Word was given first place.

The word *"sanctified"* we see in the King James Version of Acts 20:32 describes a manifestation of life produced by cooperating with the indwelling Holy Spirit. This keeps us separated from the world's system. Yes, when we were born again we were set apart or sanctified, but we must walk in that sanctification in order to receive the inheritances we have been promised. This is one reason we are to be involved with a local church and to have fellowship with those of like precious faith.

> *John 8:31-32 (NKJV)*
> *Then Jesus said to those Jews who believed Him, 'If you abide in My word, you are My disciples indeed. And you shall know the truth, and the truth shall make you free.'*

A disciple is one who follows the teaching and pattern of the life of another.

> *3 John 1:4 (NKJV)*
> *I have no greater joy than to hear that my children walk in truth.*

We are to be entrusted to God and to the word of His grace in His truth so we will be free. The results are that we are built up, and this will cause us to receive an inheritance among all those who are sanctified. John said this gave him great joy. How much joy do you think we would have if we walked in these truths? Jesus wants our joy to be full.

> *John 8:32 (NKJV)*
> *And you shall know the truth, and the truth shall make you free.*

This word *"know"* is very important. There are two other examples of this word in the New Testament that I want to bring to your attention.

> The first is in *Luke 1:34*, which says, *"Then said Mary unto the angel, How could this be, since I do not know a man?"*

The other instance is actually a number of usages in rapid succession:

> Matthew 26:70,72,74 (NKJV)
> But he denied it before them all, saying, *"I do not know what you are saying"*... But again he denied with an oath, *"I do not know the Man!"*... Then he began to curse and swear, saying, *"I do not know the Man!"*

Notice what Peter said. *"I do not know the man."* Both Mary and Peter had spent time with the Man they said they did not know. What did Mary mean when she said, *"I know not a man"*? She meant she had not had a relationship with a man that would have produced a child.

What was Peter saying? He was saying he had not been with Him to know Him in a way that would produce fruit.

To know means to have a close working relationship that produces fruit as you abide with. We must not only know the truth, but we must also abide with the truth and have a close working relationship with that truth so it will produce fruit.

Mary had the right know in relationship with the Word and the Holy Spirit that produced fruit. You and I can also have that right know with the Word and Holy Spirit that will produce fruit.

Praise God, Peter did get to a place where he had this know, for later in his life he produced much fruit.

> **Jesus wants us to know Him
> So we can produce fruit.**

Chapter Six

"Grace to Glory"

In chapter one I made reference to the Scriptures in Exodus that caused me to study more about God's grace as the doorway to revealing His glory. Let's go to back to those Scriptures and see some other things that will help us see the importance of grace to glory

> *Exodus 33:6-19 (NKJV)*
> *So the children of Israel stripped themselves of their ornaments by Mount Horeb. Moses took his tent and pitched it outside the camp, far from the camp, and called it the tabernacle of meeting. And it came to pass that everyone who sought the LORD went out to the tabernacle of meeting which was outside the camp.*
>
> *So it was, whenever Moses went out to the tabernacle, that all the people rose, and each man stood at his tent door and watched Moses until he had gone into the tabernacle. And it came to pass, when Moses entered the tabernacle, that the pillar of cloud descended and stood at the door of the*

tabernacle, and the LORD talked with Moses. All the people saw the pillar of cloud standing at the tabernacle door, and all the people rose and worshipped, each man in his tent door.

So the LORD spoke to Moses face to face, as a man speaks to his friend. And he would return to the camp, but his servant Joshua the son of Nun, a young man, did not depart from the tabernacle.

Then Moses said to the LORD, "See, You say to me, 'Bring up this people.' But You have not let me know whom You will send with me. Yet You have said, 'I know you by name, and you have also found grace in My sight.' Now therefore, I pray, if I have found grace in Your sight, show me now Your way, that I may know You and that I may find grace in Your sight. And consider that this nation is Your people."

And He said, "My Presence will go with you, and I will give you rest." Then he said to Him, "If Your Presence does not go with us, do not bring us up from here. For how then will it be known that Your people and I have found grace in Your sight, except You go with us? So we shall be separate, Your people and I, from all the people who are upon the face of the earth." So the LORD said to Moses, "I will also do this thing that you have spoken; for you have found grace in My sight, and I know you by name." And he said, "Please, show me Your glory." Then He said, "I will make all My goodness pass before you, and I will proclaim the name of the LORD before you. I will be gracious to whom I will be gracious, and I will have compassion on whom I will have compassion."

Exodus then goes on to say the following:

Exodus 34:5-6 (NKJV)
Now the LORD descended in the cloud and stood with him there, and proclaimed the name of the LORD. And the LORD passed before him and proclaimed, "The LORD, the LORD God, merciful and gracious, longsuffering, and abounding in goodness and truth..."

The more I study and come to understand, the more I am convinced that God's grace toward man (and manifesting through man) is a major key to helping others see the glory of God. God's grace flowed down from heaven through a man named Jesus, who allowed that grace to flow through Him to every type of person you could imagine. Just think about the type of people who came to Jesus—the rich, the poor, the sick, the demon possessed, the beggars, the blind, the deaf, the foolish and the wise. Even the cheaters and liars came to Him, and each person had the opportunity to receive that amazing grace.

Most people that are born again come to Christ because someone operated in this grace and introduced them to God's saving grace. That is a great thing, but God's grace is not to stop at salvation and is to grow and multiply in us and through us to help others receive grace and grow in that same grace and truth in turn. In *Acts 4:33*, we read that great grace was upon them. Then in *Acts 11:23, Barnabus saw the grace of God upon the believers in Antioch.*

In *Exodus 33:12,* God said to Moses, *"I know you by name and you have also found grace in my sight."* If you are a child of God, He knows you by name and you have found grace in His sight. If you are not a child of God, you can receive that grace now by calling on the name of the Lord to be saved. You do this by faith.

Moses continued talking to God and said, *"If I have found grace in Your sight, show me now Your way, that I may know You and that I may find grace in Your sight. And consider that this nation is Your people"* (Exodus 33:13 NKJV). Moses had already found the grace of God, but He wanted more. As you learn the definitions of grace, you will also want more—not only for yourself but also for others.

Note in verse thirteen Moses wanted to include the people. God's answer to Moses' request was, *"My presence shall go with thee."* In verse fifteen, Moses tells God, *"If Your presence does not go with us do not bring us up from here."* Remember, the Lord is talking to Moses as a friend, and the Lord tells Moses, *"I will do this thing you have asked of me. I will go with you and you will know my presence."*

After it settled in Moses' heart, he asked the Lord to show him His glory, and the Lord did.

If you read this story carefully, you will notice that most of the conversation between the Lord and Moses took place outside the tabernacle. It started in the tabernacle, but Moses turned and went back into the camp, and Joshua stayed in the tabernacle. You and I can get it started in church, but we are to continue to talk with God as a friend throughout the camp of our lives.

Inside the tabernacle, Moses and the people saw a cloudy pillar at the door. Outside the tabernacle when God showed Moses His glory, what did he see? God's goodness.

Read *Exodus 34:6* and you will see that the glory of the Lord was made up of the Lord's mercy, graciousness, and long-suffering, and it was abundant in goodness and truth. It seems to me that everything we need in life is summed up in these words about God's glory:

> *Exodus 34:6*
> *And the LORD passed before him and proclaimed, 'The LORD, the LORD God, merciful and gracious, longsuffering, and abounding in goodness and truth...'*

There are reasons why we do not see the glory of God. One reason is the devil has blinded our eyes from seeing. But before we blame it on the devil let's see another reason. The other reason we are not seeing this glory is that we are not walking in the grace of God like we should.

One of the things I see we in the Body of Christ need is revival. I have heard about this word *"revival"* all of my life. When I was young, every spring the local churches had revival meetings, but nothing much happened. When I first went into the ministry, I was a lay pastor and studying at Emory University preparing to be a Methodist pastor. We also had what was called revival meetings, and about the only thing that happened was that a few people would recommit their lives to the Lord. These meetings were not what you call wrong, but I believe God had more in mind for revival than that.

Let's not try to correct the whole Church as to why there is not a revival. Let's examine our own lives. Check to see if you are walking in the grace of God to the point it is flowing through you to those around you for them to see and experience. Let's have a revival of grace to show forth His glory. We do need grace to be continually revived in our hearts and actions.

I know the word revival is used in many different ways. People pray for revival, and at the same time pray for a mighty outpouring of the Holy Spirit. We need both because they support each other. When there is a mighty outpouring of the Holy Spirit, people should be revived. Yet at the same time, often there is not a mighty outpouring of the Holy Spirit because people have not been revived. When one is properly revived, one can help set the stage for an outpouring of the Holy Ghost so others will see the glory of God and come into the Kingdom of the family of God.

When we are properly revived, we will show forth His glory.

What does *"revival"* mean, and who is it for? Webster's New World Dictionary says that revival is bringing or coming back to use; a restoration to vigor or activity. It's a return to life, and it can also be a stirring up of religious faith. Revival is for those who were once on fire for the things of God but have become lackluster in their walk with Him.

It was God's grace through faith that gave you the new life, (a new power alignment) in Christ Jesus. We call that saving grace. God the Father, through His Son, made it available to us. Praise God, He even gave us the faith to activate that grace. But guess what? We are to grow in this grace, and it is to be multiplied in us and through us. That saving grace is not to just sit on the shelves of our heart. God did not give us grace as a souvenir. He gave it as a gift. Souvenirs remind us of special happenings of the past. Grace is a gift, and gifts are for the benefit of the one who receives them. When we activate the gift of grace properly, it will bring glory to God and benefit both others and us.

I want to insert two Scriptures. The first is *Psalms 85:6*, which says, *"Wilt thou not revive us again: that thy people may rejoice in thee?"* The answer to this Scripture is yes, if we ask Him to.

The second is *Psalms 138:7-8*, which says, *"Though I walk in the midst of trouble, thou wilt revive me: thou shalt stretch forth thine hand against the wrath of mine enemies, and thy right hand shall save me. The LORD will perfect that which concerneth me: thy mercy, O LORD, endureth for ever: forsake not the works of thine own hands."*

Stand on these two Scripture promises, and God will bring about great results. When we make the decision to ask God to revive us, He stretches forth His hand to protect us and saves us. Protection is great, but being perfected while you are protected is something else. For when we are being perfected, we are being restored.

The writer of this Psalm is asking the Lord not to forsake the works of His hands, but in all reality the Lord never did forsake the work of His hands. It was us that forsook His hands. For the Lord God to revive us, we must stay in His hands. He will not forsake the works of His hands. But what happens is that we start wiggling in the flesh and slip out of His hand.

So when you pray, don't just pray for revival—ask the Lord by His Word and the Holy Ghost to revive you. And then let Him do it. When this process starts, you will find yourself in revival.

> "Revive us in your grace for your glory, Lord."

Chapter Seven

"Jesus with Grace"

The grace of God is supremely revealed and given in the person and work of *JESUS CHRIST*.

Jesus was not only the beneficiary of God's grace; He was the very embodiment of it, bringing it to man for salvation by His death and resurrection.

This word *"salvation"* includes the complete recovery and the complete restoration of man. The work of grace flowing through Jesus to us was never intended to just get us into heaven and nothing else. We are required to grow in this grace until every aspect of the human life is restored to its original standard or form of being.

It is an established truth that we were saved by faith according to *Ephesians 2:8*. Jesus not only became poor spiritually in order for us to become new creatures in Him but He also because of the grace of God, became poor in order that we may be made rich.

2 Corinthians 5:17 (NKJV)
Therefore, if anyone is in Christ, he is a new creation; old things have passed away; behold, all things have become new.

2 Corinthians 8:9 (NKJV)
For you know the grace of our Lord Jesus Christ, that though He was rich, yet for your sakes He became poor, that you through His poverty might become rich.

Remember what it tells us in John's Gospel?

John 1:14,16-17 (NKJV)
And the Word became flesh and dwelt among us, and we beheld His glory, the glory as of the only begotten of the Father, full of grace and truth... And of His fullness we have all received, and grace for grace. For the law was given through Moses, but grace and truth came through Jesus Christ.

John 1:16 (NIV)
From the fullness of his grace we have all received one blessing after another.

Now as we desire to see the glory of God, notice what it says about what the glory looks like: it was full of grace and truth.

The Word of God is a glorious Gospel, and, when we have revelation of it by the Holy Ghost, we are seeing the glory of the Lord.

> *2 Corinthians 4:4 (NKJV)*
> *Whose minds the god of this age has blinded, who do not believe, lest the light of the gospel of the glory of Christ, who is the image of God, should shine on them.*

Before people are born again, their minds are dark—void of light. But when they call on the name of the Lord to be saved, the glorious Gospel illuminates their minds. That is a most glorious thing! They saw the glory of God and let it in.

I love *1 Timothy 1:11-12*. It is a wonderful thing to be trusted with the glorious Gospel of the Lord Jesus Christ and to be counted faithful with that Gospel causing one to be in the ministry.

> *1 Timothy 1:11-12 (NKJV)*
> *According to the glorious gospel of the blessed God, which was committed to my trust. Glory to God for His Grace and I thank Christ Jesus our Lord who has enabled me, because He counted me faithful, putting me into the ministry.*

Back to *2 Corinthians 8:9* which says, *"For you know the grace of our Lord Jesus Christ, that though He was rich, yet for your sakes He became poor, that you through His poverty might be rich."*

Paul said something very interesting here. He said, *"For we know."* Know what? The grace of the Lord Jesus Christ. What do you know about the grace of the Lord Jesus Christ? I believe after reading this book, you will know more, but do you know about the grace of the Lord Jesus Christ? Do you know that though He was rich, for your sake He became poor, so that through His being made poor of His own free will, you and I would be made rich?

When Jesus went to the cross and died He became poor not just spiritually, but He became bankrupt mentally, physically, and spiritually. He became:

- Dead for you to have life;
- Sad so you could have joy;
- Sick so you could become well;
- Lonely so you would not be alone;
- Dumb so you could have wisdom;
- Oppressed so you could think;
- Poor so you could become rich in all things;
- He gave up grace so you could have it;
- He gave up His position so you could have a position;
- He gave up righteousness so you could have righteousness;
- He gave up love so you could have love and be loving;

- He gave up the keys to the Kingdom so you could have the keys;
- He gave up the Spirit so you could have His;
- He gave up His glory so you could have it;
- He gave up all that was His so you could have all that He had.

Yes, He gave up all these things and more. But when the Father saw that all had been paid for and Jesus had taken it all, He said, "That is it! The price has been paid. I am giving Him back everything so all things pertaining to life and godliness will be available to man." Praise God, it is ours! All we have to do is receive it by faith in love. Why is this true? Because Jesus took the keys from the devil and gave those keys to the Church—those who have called on the name of the Lord to be saved.

I will make a comment here just to get you to thinking. Jesus took keys and gave keys. Keys do two things. They lock and they unlock. According to the Bible, we have the authority to bind and loose. This book is about grace, and as you will read, you will see what locks up grace and what unlocks grace. You will see what binds it, or hinders it, and what looses it. This is determined by what keys we use. Not all keys are from Jesus. The flesh has keys and the devil has keys.

So whose keys are you using?

Remember we have been saved by grace through faith. We are to live by faith and stand in grace and grow in grace. We are to reign in this life through Jesus Christ by God's abundant provision of grace and the gift of righteousness.

There is a very interesting Scripture in *Luke 4:22* which says, *"So all bore witness to Him, and marveled at the gracious words which proceeded out of His mouth."* What kind of words? Gracious words. Why were they gracious words? Because Jesus was full of grace and truth.

It is also interesting that these words were spoken about Jesus right after He had declared this about Himself and the ministry He was to have:

Luke 4:18-19 (NKJV)
The Spirit of the LORD is upon Me, Because He has anointed Me To preach the gospel to the poor; He has sent Me to heal the brokenhearted, To proclaim liberty to the captives And recovery of sight to the blind, To set at liberty those who are oppressed; To proclaim the acceptable year of the LORD.

Jesus could speak these words because He was full of grace and truth and He stayed in that grace and truth. The first man, Adam, had this grace and truth also, but he did not stay in it. Remember, in the beginning of Genesis, God made man in His own image.

So you and I have received this grace. We have truth, and we can grow in grace and truth—causing us to speak graciously and with power like Jesus. But the problem has been especially present with me in my early years: we are often more full of truth than grace.

Jesus was a man who walked the face of this earth full of the Holy Ghost, full of grace, and full of the truth.

Notice what it says in *Matthew 7:28-29: "And so it was, when Jesus had ended these sayings, that the people were astonished at His teaching, for He taught them as one having authority, and not as the scribes"*

In Luke chapter four we saw where the people wondered or were astonished at His doctrine, for He spoke so graciously. But in Matthew chapter seven, they are astonished at His teachings because He taught with authority—truth.

Why did I bring out these two verses of Scripture about speaking graciously and with authority? Because they go hand-in-hand. When one is full of grace and truth, he or she will speak with grace and authority.

Perhaps you have noticed that you can speak more graciously about a subject you know a lot about compared to things you know little about. When you know a lot about something, you can speak with authority.

Jesus was full of grace and truth, and He spoke with authority.

Jesus said, *"And you shall know the truth, and the truth shall make you free" (John 8:32).*

> **Know the truth; then speak graciously with authority.**

Chapter Eight

"Grace in the Book of Acts"

I believe the Book of Acts is a pattern of how the Church is to operate. Most of my Christian life, I have heard different examples of revival and the outpouring of the Holy Ghost in the last days. Many believers have researched past revivals and outpourings of the Holy Ghost, with the signs and wonders God did through those spiritual events. Many powerful words have been brought to our attention for us to believe and act on to see revival and outpourings of the Holy Ghost.

Sometimes it seems to me like we get to thinking about the big picture of God's work over the years, and we overlook what is taking place in the lives of those Spirit-filled, Bible-believing Christians who are doing the works of Jesus. Thousands of people all over the world are seeing revival and mighty outpourings of the Holy Ghost with signs and wonders.

I remember years ago a pastor friend and I were talking about revival, and he said, "I see revival in this church and town each week. Each week, I see people get turned back on for Jesus. Each week, I see someone born again or healed." Then he said, "We are in revival all the time." At the time we were talking, his church was very small. Today it has over a thousand people, and it has missionaries in many countries.

As I have read of revivals and outpourings of the Holy Ghost in the past (and especially in the oldest report I know about the Book of Acts), I am convinced mighty revival and outpourings of the Holy Ghost must have within them a mighty ingredient called grace.

Let's look into the Book of Acts and see what they did and what people saw in regards to this grace. As you read this chapter about grace in the book of Acts, keep in mind the things we have learned about grace. I believe this look at grace in the Book of Acts is necessary and the Scriptures will support themselves. I am not going to say a lot about these examples, but just bring them to your attention.

> *Acts 4:33 (NKJV)*
> *And with great power the apostles gave witness to the resurrection of the Lord Jesus. And great grace was upon them all.*

What were the ingredients they had working in their lives that caused there to be great grace on all of them? Number one, most of them had been baptized with the Holy Ghost with the evidence of speaking in tongues and had received the power or ability to witness. Number two; they knew the story of God's gracious plan of redemption. It seems like each time they preached, they started from the beginning up to now. Number three, as they used the power and ability they had received on the Day of Pentecost, it did what Jude said it would do. Note the two following Scriptures. (Every time I think of the first one, I think of the second one. To me they go together like a horse and carriage.)

> *Acts 1:8 (NKJV)*
> *But you shall receive power when the Holy Spirit has come upon you; and you shall be witnesses to Me in Jerusalem, and in all Judea and Samaria, and to the end of the earth."*
>
> *Jude 20-22 (NKJV)*
> *But you, beloved, building yourselves up on your most holy faith, praying in the Holy Spirit, keep yourselves in the love of God, looking for the mercy of our Lord Jesus Christ unto eternal life. And on some have compassion, making a distinction.*

Why is this so important? Because when you pray in the Holy Ghost, you are building up yourself as you use your faith to stay in the love of God. The love of God is full of grace. When someone is full of the Spirit, they are full of love and full of grace.

When you are full of these things, you will testify of the resurrected Lord. If we are not testifying of the

Lord and the power of His resurrection, we are not full. So I suggest we stay in a place of praying in the Holy Ghost until we are full—so full it pours out not just in church but also in the streets and byways where the sinners are.

The Bible tells us it is the goodness of the Lord that causes one to repent: *Romans 2:4 says, "...knowing that the goodness of God leads you to repent."* Remember, in the beginning of this book we saw one of the things in the glory of God was goodness.

We know that Jesus is our perfect example and this is what Peter said about our example. He said it in *Acts 10:38, "How God anointed Jesus of Nazareth with the Holy Spirit and with power, who went about doing good and healing all who were oppressed by the devil, for God was with Him" (NKJV).* We have the same Holy Ghost and power as those in the Book of Acts, meaning we can do good and heal and deliver those oppressed by the devil.

What we need to get clear in our lives is the power to do good, which is listed here before healing and deliverance. This is why this grace is of so much importance. Because when we walk in grace, we are doing good, thereby setting the stage for the power of God to flow. This is our part. It is the necessary part for those sick and needing deliverance to see this grace and draw from it. As we see in the Book of Acts, the people saw this grace and they called it grace. In the last part of Act 10:38, it says this is when God will be with us to the point of manifesting His power for healing and deliverance.

This great power they had in Acts chapter four was the power of the Holy Ghost, which gave them the ability to do good and testify of the resurrected Lord. They did it to the point that great grace was upon them all. If they did it, we can too. We have the same power or ability, because we have the same Holy Ghost, and we have the same resurrected Lord.

Acts 11:23 (NKJV)
When he came and had seen the grace of God, he was glad, and encouraged them all that with purpose of heart they should continue with the Lord.

The "he" in this Scripture is Barnabas. It tells us he saw the grace of God. What was it about this grace he saw? What happened for him to be able to see it? At the beginning of this chapter, Peter was telling them what had happened to him in chapter ten. This whole story took place because men were praying and had a desire to receive and do the things of God.

In *Acts 10:2* it tells us Cornelius was a man of prayer, plus he was a giver. In *Acts 10:9*, Peter was on the housetop praying. The first man wanted understanding on how to get saved; the second man was a preacher who knew how to share the Gospel. As the two were praying, the Holy Ghost moved, giving both of them instructions on what to do. Praise God, they both followed the instructions and the saving Gospel of the Lord Jesus was made available to the Gentiles.

After this happened, Peter went back to Jerusalem and told them what had happened, because they got on his case for going before what they considered unclean people. But after they heard about the goodness of the Lord to save the Gentiles, it tells us in verse eighteen, *"When they heard these things they became silent; and they glorified God, saying,"* Then God has also granted *to the Gentiles repentance to life"* (Acts 11:18 NKJV).

Keep reading in verses nineteen to twenty-two, where it tells us:

> *Acts 11:19-22 (NKJV)*
> *Now those who were scattered after the persecution that arose over Stephen traveled as far as Phoenicia, Cyprus, and Antioch, preaching the word to no one but the Jews only. But some of them were men from Cyprus and Cyrene, who, when they had come to Antioch, spoke to the Hellenists, preaching the Lord Jesus. And the hand of the Lord was with them, and a great number believed and turned to the Lord. Then news of these things came to the ears of the church in Jerusalem, and they sent out Barnabas to go as far as Antioch.*

And the hand of the Lord was with them: and a great number believed, and turned unto the Lord. Then tidings of these things came unto the ears of the church, which was in Jerusalem: and they sent forth Barnabas that he should go as far as Antioch.

Here they are scattered abroad, but they are preaching the Lord Jesus Christ. The result was manifested grace that others could see. Note in chapter ten and eleven, the only sign and wonders are salvation experiences for men and women. Yes, there were manifestations of the Spirit to Cornelius as he prayed and to Peter as he prayed. Then the Holy Ghost confirmed the word with signs—people being saved.

What did Barnabas see? He saw the saving grace of God, the greatest sign and wonder of them all, the miracle of all miracles—the grace to be saved.

The next place we see the word grace in the Book of Acts is in Acts chapter thirteen.

Acts 13:43 (NKJV)
Now when the congregation had broken up, many of the Jews and devout proselytes followed Paul and Barnabas, who, speaking to them, persuaded them to continue in the grace of God.

My question is, "How do you persuade someone to continue in the grace of God?" We can see the answer to this question if we go back and read Acts 13:14 where

Paul was preaching to the Jews in the synagogue. Paul shared with them about the Hebrew children being delivered from Egypt all the way to Jesus' resurrection.

Then *Acts 13:42* shows the Gentiles wanting this Gospel of grace. The next Sabbath day came, and almost the whole city gathered together to hear the Word of God. Then the Jews came against Paul, but Paul and Barnabas grew bold and said, *"It was necessary that the word of God should be spoken to you first: but seeing ye put it from you, and judge yourselves unworthy of everlasting life, lo, we turn to the Gentiles" (Acts 13:46).*

What were Paul and Barnabas saying? They were telling us to preach the Word of God and to preach it until we find someone who will listen. These Jews would not, so they went to the Gentiles.

If you desire to persuade someone to continue in the grace of God, share with him or her the Word—the story of God's plan of total redemption.

In the passages we have looked at up to this point in the book of Acts, there were no healings or miracles other than people being born again. Yet this is the greatest miracle. Yes, there were signs and wonders done in earlier chapters, but I am talking about these chapters where grace was mentioned.

Now, in chapter fourteen we will see that there were signs and wonders in connection to this grace:

Acts 14:1-3 (NKJV)
Now it happened in Iconium that they went together to the synagogue of the Jews, and so spoke that a great multitude both of the Jews and of the Greeks believed. But the unbelieving Jews stirred up the Gentiles and poisoned their minds against the brethren. Therefore they stayed there a long time, speaking boldly in the Lord, who was bearing witness to the word of His grace, granting signs and wonders to be done by their hands.

Paul and Barnabas went up together and spoke to a great multitude of both Jews and Gentiles, but, as always, there were some unbelievers who stirred up trouble. Notice what Paul and Barnabas did: For a long time they stayed and spoke boldly in the Lord, giving testimony of His grace. When we go and preach in the Lord (in the Spirit), grace will manifest to save and heal with signs and wonders following.

The word grace is used six more times in the book of Acts. I suggest you look them up and study them, but there are two I will mention here:

Acts 20:24 (NKJV)
But none of these things move me; nor do I count my life dear to myself, so that I may finish my race with joy, and the ministry which I received from the Lord Jesus, to testify to the gospel of the grace of God.

Notice what Paul said his ministry was—to testify to the Gospel of the grace of God. Paul is saying goodbye to the people to whom he had been preaching. Verse thirty-two is a very powerful verse. He is commending them to God and to the word of His grace. Well, if they can be commended to God and to the Word of His grace, we can be too.

Paul did not just stop at commending them to God and His Word of grace. He went on to tell them what this grace would do. It will do two things: It will build you up, and it will give you an inheritance.

> **His grace was sufficient for Paul and others.**
> **His grace is sufficient for us.**

Chapter Nine

"Three Kinds of Glory"

There are three operations or kinds of glory mentioned in the Word of God. We love to talk and tell of the glory of God, but many do not walk in His glory because they are trying to please God with their walk of glory in the flesh.

> *1 Corinthians 1:29-31 (NKJV)*
> *That no flesh should glory in His presence. But of Him you are in Christ Jesus, who became for us wisdom from God — and righteousness and sanctification and redemption   that, as it is written, "He who glories, let him glory in the LORD."*

> *2 Corinthians 11:18 (NKJV)*
> *Seeing that many boast according to the flesh, I also will boast.*

> *Galatians 6:12-14 (NKJV)*
> *As many as desire to make a good showing in the flesh, these would compel you to be circumcised, only that they may not suffer persecution for the*

cross of Christ. For not even those who are circumcised keep the law, but they desire to have you circumcised that they may boast in your flesh. But God forbid that I should boast except in the cross of our Lord Jesus Christ, by whom the world has been crucified to me, and I to the world.

First Corinthians 1:29-31 plainly tells us *"no flesh shall glory in His presence,"* but if we want to glory, let us glory in the Lord.

This *"glory or boasting in the Lord"* is not all about how you dress, use makeup, wear expensive jewelry, or drive a special car. It is not about you boasting about what you have done. It is boasting about what Jesus has done. It has to do with the attitude of the heart. I believe we are to dress nicely and cleanly in representing the Lord on a daily basis and when we attend church and special meetings. I believe we are to drive nice, clean cars. I believe we can boast in how we have been used by God, but we must make sure it was the things of God flowing through us and not just us

But if the attitude is, "I want to be decked out and drive the finest so people will see how glorious I am," you are in the flesh. A word that comes to me as I write this is the word pride. This word is fleshly and can become demonic—or it can be a Christian pride and make one stronger in the Lord.

Maybe asking a question would help us understand this: Are you proud to be a Christian, or are you more proud about your outward appearance? If I stand before God trying to impress Him and others with the way I am dressed, I am glorying in the flesh, and it will not work with God.

A prime example of this is seen in the life of Lucifer, who was one of the three angels mentioned by name in the Bible. In heaven he was the one dressed in all the beautiful things. The Scriptures below describe him, and I want you to see how much he had—but that was not what God saw. It was the attitude and motive of his heart that God noticed. Because, as you can see, when his heart, attitude, and disposition changed, he still had all the beautiful things. It was pride that caused him not to be able to stand in the presence of God. The results were he was out.

Ezekiel 28:13-19
You were in Eden, the garden of God; Every precious stone was your covering: The sardius, topaz, and diamond, Beryl, onyx, and jasper, Sapphire, turquoise, and emerald with gold. The workmanship of your timbrels and pipes Was prepared for you on the day you were created.

You were the anointed cherub who covers; I established you; You were on the holy mountain of God; You walked back and forth in the midst of fiery stones. You were perfect in your ways from the day you were created, Till iniquity was found in you.

By the abundance of your trading You became filled with violence within, And you sinned; Therefore I cast you as a profane thing Out of the mountain of God; And I destroyed you, O covering cherub, From the midst of the fiery stones." Your heart was lifted up because of your beauty; You corrupted your wisdom for the sake of your splendor; I cast you to the ground, I laid you before kings, That they might gaze at you.

You defiled your sanctuaries By the multitude of your iniquities, By the iniquity of your trading; Therefore I brought fire from your midst; It devoured you, And I turned you to ashes upon the earth In the sight of all who saw you. All who knew you among the peoples are astonished at you; You have become a horror, And shall be no more forever.

Back to this concept of fleshly glory. Hollywood is full of fleshly glory. It is not only Hollywood; people all over the world are weighted down with the things of the flesh—both in the natural and in the spirit. They have become heavy with the things of the flesh to the point where they don't even want God, much less to stand in His presence.

This is why we need to watch over our hearts and guard them so that when God blesses our lives and adds materialistic things to us, we don't get sidetracked into pride.

What does *1 Corinthians 1:30* say? Let's read it again. *"But of him are ye in Christ Jesus, who of God is made unto us wisdom, and righteousness, and sanctification, and redemption."*

If we are going to live and walk a life that is glorious and brings honor to Him, we will have to have *1 Corinthians 1:30* functioning in our lives. When we walk in God's wisdom, His righteousness, His sanctification, and His redemptive power, we will not be walking in the flesh but in the Spirit. Then we are glorying in Him before His presence.

Note, *2 Corinthians 10:17* says, *"But he that glorieth, let him glory in the Lord."*

Now the question is, how did Paul glory in the Lord? To better understand this, let's look at some of the definitions of glory. Glory equals boasting (in a good way) is taking joy, or rejoicing in something. It's a good opinion of God's attributes, ways, and power. It's giving honor. Boasting might be saying, "He is my Father, He is my Lord, He is my healer, He is my provider." Yes, we who claim to be faith people say these are positive confessions, and they are, but they are also truths of boasting in the Lord, or glorying in the Lord.

Paul gloried in the Lord by boasting about who God was, what He had done, what He was doing, what He will do. Paul also said something else that was quite interesting.

> *2 Corinthians 12:9*
> *And he said unto me, My grace is sufficient for thee: for my strength is made perfect in weakness. Most gladly therefore will I rather glory in my infirmities, that the power of Christ may rest upon me.*

Note that Paul says two distinct things. The first one is that God told him, "My grace is sufficient for thee." The second is, "I rather glory in my infirmities." The second one is one of the things that make the first one work. What is Paul saying here? He is saying, "I am going to boast, brag on, lift up, and exhort the Lord above all things. Above my infirmities. Above my situation. Above everything."

The decision to boast in the Lord is what helps keep Paul's eyes and heart on the Lord, setting the stage for God's grace and glory to manifest.

I have said there were three operations or kinds of glory. We just looked at one of them—the glory of the flesh. Now, let's see about the second one, the devil's glory. I made some mention of the devil's ways already, but there is one word that sums up his glory and that of the flesh: pride.

One of the definitions of glory is to be weighted down heavily, and there is one thing pride will do—weight you down and destroy you.

Let me bring your attention to where the Bible tells us about Jesus being tempted by the devil. I do hope you understand Jesus was not the first or last person the devil tempted.

Matthew 4:8 (NKJV)
Again, the devil took Him up on an exceedingly high mountain, and showed Him all the kingdoms of the world and their glory.

The devil is called the god of this world, and he has blinded the eyes of far too many people. One of the ways he has done this is by influencing them to fall into his glory—the glory of the world. Some may be reading this and say, "Well, that is just the flesh." It starts there, but when one walks in the flesh long enough, it makes way for demonic control. It becomes a weighty heaviness that is hard to break away from. The blood of Jesus and the Word of God can break it. But the truth is, we do not have to fall into it at all if we recognize the devil's trap of glory and turn it down the way Jesus did.

How did Jesus turn down the devil's glory of this world? *Matthew 4:10* tells us that Jesus said, *"Away with you, Satan! For it is written, 'You shall worship the LORD your God, and Him only you shall serve.'"*

Jesus did it the same way you and I can—by worshipping the Lord our God and by serving Him. *James 4:6-7* says, *"But He gives more grace. Therefore He says: 'God resists the proud, but gives grace to the humble.' Therefore submit to God. Resist the devil and he will flee from you" (NKJV).*

One submits to God by worshipping Him, by reading His Word, and by praying in the Holy Ghost. One also submits to God by serving in the local church and reaching others with the saving Gospel of the Lord Jesus Christ.

The moment you submitted to God, you started the process of resisting the devil. Yet the moment you submit to the flesh and the devil, you start the progress of resisting God. So, let's just submit to the Word of God and the Holy Spirit!

Now the third operation or kind of glory is the glory of the Lord. Let's refresh the definition of glory. Glory is: "to be heavy, be weighty, to be honored. To show one's self mighty or great. To be wealthy. To be rich."

We saw how the weight of the flesh can cause us to be unable to stand in the presence of the Lord. But there is something else about the weight of the flesh I need to bring to your attention.

Countless people have fallen into the trap of glorying in the flesh, trying to look more glorious than someone else—trying to keep up with the Jones family and their glorious stuff. People go into debt to do it, and it becomes a weighty and heavy thing to them—to the extent some end up losing all they have.

There is a way out of this mess, and it is by repenting and asking God for mercy. Then live your life in a way that brings glory to God rather than giving glory to self and the flesh.

What is so amazing about the glory of the Lord, the one that is of most importance, is that we who are children of God have it. We also have His grace. We also have the faith to activate this grace to be able live a life to bring glory to God.

Look at these two Scriptures:

Colossians 1:27 (NKJV)
To them God willed to make known what are the riches of the glory of this mystery among the Gentiles: which is Christ in you, the hope of glory.

John 17:22 (NKJV)
And the glory, which You gave Me I have given them, that they may be one just as We are one.

Also look at this passage:

2 Peter 1:3-4 (NKJV)
As His divine power has given to us all things that pertain to life and godliness, through the knowledge of Him who called us by glory and virtue, by which have been given to us exceedingly great and precious promises, that through these you may be partakers of the divine nature, having escaped the corruption that is in the world through lust.

The glory and all divine power have been given to us and with in this glory and divine power is everything that pertains to life and godliness. We receive it by the knowledge of Him that called us to glory. But when you are called or asked to do or be something, you must receive knowledge about what you are to do or be.

See what *2 Peter 1:4* tells us: We were given exceedingly great and precious promises so that we might be partakers of His divine nature, which cause us to escape the corruption of the world through lust. This lust is just a desiring of other things more than God's things. It is a walk that wants to glorify self more than God.

We have precious promises that will meet our physical needs, both in healing and prosperity. But we have far more precious promises that cause Christ in us, the hope of glory, to come forth and bring glory to the King of Kings and Lord of Lords.

So, my friend, become so weighted down with the Word of God and His Spirit that it pushes all the works of the flesh out of your system and leaves no place for the devil and his glory. Then we must stay full of God so our lives continually bring glory to God.

This glory of the Lord that is so weighty and heavy will have the very opposite effect of the weight of the flesh, sin, and the devil. Without the glory of the Lord, the weight of the flesh, sin, and the devil can become so heavy one cannot carry it; instead, it crushes us.

But, praise the Lord, the weight of the things of God makes things lighter and lighter. Why? Because they are the things of God. The things of God carry more weight than the things of the flesh and devil. So my friend, release the weight of the Lord upon those things in your life that are hindering you from experiencing His glory.

> **Let grace arise to show forth His glory**

Chapter Ten

"Grace to You for Others"

Most of the teaching in this book has been focused on God's grace towards us for us to be more Christ-like in His grace and to be made fit for the Master's use. I hope you know and understand the reason God wants us to be Christ-like in our walk of grace. It is so we can be good stewards of the manifold grace of God.

When I received Christ as my Lord in November 1969, I read my first chapter of Scripture. It was *1 Peter 4*. Verse ten in the Living Bible says, *"God has given each of you some special abilities; be sure to use them to help each other, passing on to others God's many kinds of blessings" (TLB).*

Here is the verse in some other translations:

1 Peter 4:10 (NKJV)
As each one has received a gift, minister it to one another, as good stewards of the manifold grace of God.

1 Peter 4:10 (MSG)
Be generous with the different things God gave you, passing them around so all get in on it.

1 Peter 4:10 (AMP)
As each of you has received a gift (a particular spiritual talent, a gracious divine endowment), employ it for one another as [befits] good trustees of God's many-sided grace [faithful stewards of the extremely diverse powers and gifts granted to Christians by unmerited favor].

After reading this verse in the Message Bible and the Amplified Bible, there is not too much left to explain about this grace to help others. God gave us this grace, and He expects us to be good stewards—to allow it to flow in us and through us to help others.

Let's look at the definition of grace once more. Grace is God's divine influence acting in man, bringing forth favorable results. Grace works to bring God's purposes to manifestation through the willing response of men to His grace. Grace also brings us into a new power alignment.

Why would God want His divine influence acting in man? First, it brings about favorable results for you and your household. Second, grace enables you to serve Him and minister to others. But the bottom line is that God must get grace to us in order to get it through us to bless someone else. We cannot give someone something we do not have.

For example, He must get money to us before He can get it through us so we can bless someone else. The same thing is true of anything else God has for mankind. He likes to use people to reach people. He wants to use you to reach people. He wants to use me to reach people.

Remember in the preface of this book where we saw God has things set up so we can be equipped to walk in love and faith to do the work of the ministry? This thing about grace is just another big attribute of His love towards people, and He wants to use us to deliver it. We are to be containers of the things of God so they can be poured upon the lives of people for them to be blessed.

In the different translations of *1 Peter 4:10* we saw some very important words that we need to be mindful of. The first of these words was "gift." Each one of us has received a gift from God. I am not just talking about gifts that cause us to be Christians and to receive. I am talking about gifts to be used for building His Church. All of us are to be building the Church. Yes, we all have a place where we fit, and while we are in that place that fits, we are to be active in helping others fit.

You may say, "I do not have a gift, a spiritual talent, or a divine endowment." But I say, "Yes you do!" Just like in the building of the tabernacle in the Old Testament, there was something every person had and could do to participate.

I did not want this chapter to be very long, but I need to get the point across. If I were preaching, I would ask for a few more minutes but now I am asking for a few more pages.

Take a look at the following Scriptures and you will see you have a special gift from God. I believe in these following Scriptures one can see any individual's gift. But before you read them, let's remember the gifts are not for you to pick and choose—they are as the Lord decides. Read and study these Scriptures prayerfully and you will see....?

> *1 Corinthians 12:28 (NKJV)*
> *And God has appointed these in the church: first apostles, second prophets, third teachers, after that miracles, then gifts of healings, helps, administrations, varieties of tongues.*

> *Romans 12:5-8 (NKJV)*
> *So we, being many, are one body in Christ, and individually members of one another. Having then gifts differing according to the grace that is given to us, let us use them: if prophecy, let us prophesy in proportion to our faith; or ministry, let us use it in our ministering; he who teaches, in teaching; he who exhorts, in exhortation; he who gives, with liberality; he who leads, with diligence; he who shows mercy, with cheerfulness.*

> *1 Corinthians 12:7-10 (NKJV)*
> *But the manifestation of the Spirit is given to each one for the profit of all: for to one is given the word of wisdom through the Spirit, to another the word of knowledge through the same Spirit, to another faith by the same Spirit, to another gifts of healings by the same Spirit, to another the working of miracles, to another prophecy, to another discerning of spirits, to another different kinds of tongues, to another the interpretation of tongues.*

You may just need to sit down and look back on your life and see what areas you have been the most comfortable in when helping people. Also, look at the area that produces the most joy and peace. This is what I did years ago, and it helped me greatly.

I was trying to be a gift for attention rather than be the gift God had in mind. To help you understand, let me tell you what I dealt with: I was trying to push being an evangelist when I am actually a teacher. I do the work of an evangelist as a believer. I do many other things as a believer, but my gift is that of a teacher. I would rather teach a class than to eat when I am hungry.

Now, let us look at another word we need to see clearly. This word is *"steward" (or "trustee")*. A steward is one who actively directs what he has been given. Well, what are we called be good stewards of? We are to watch over and use wisely the gifts that God has given us, whether it is a gift for your own personal well being, for another, or for a group. It may be a gift such as love, faith, grace, the Holy Spirit, etc., or a special gift or talent that is listed in the Scriptures above.

We are to be loyal in using the gifts God has given us. What I mean by being loyal is using the gift the way God wants it used and using it when and where God wants it used. It is being totally committed to Him and His way.

The last words in these Scriptures we need to look at are *"the manifold grace of God."* Have you every noticed that many times throughout the Bible, things of nature or man-made things were use as an analogy for us to better see something that was being said. Well, I want to do this with this word *"manifold"* in *1 Peter 4:10*.

As I think about this word *"manifold,"* knowing what it means in this scripture, I also think about the manifolds on an engine. With this thought in mind, I want to just briefly use the analogy of the manifold on an engine compared with manifold grace of God.

In the beginning of this chapter we made reference to four different translations of 1 Peter 4:10. When I see the overview of these verses, I think of the manifolds on an engine.

Now as you may know there are thousands of different kind of engines and thousands of different kinds of manifolds for those engines. Think about it: there are thousands upon thousands of different kinds of people with the manifold grace of God upon their lives.

Still talking about the engine, let me tell you what an engine is. An engine is any machine that uses energy to develop mechanical power. (Webster's New World Dictionary) We as God's engines should use the energy of God's Word to produce spiritual power.

So what is it about an engine that I think of when I think about the manifold grace of God? Well first, engines have manifolds and on these engines, manifolds are used to distribute things into the engine and out of the engine. We as Christians are to be distributors of the manifold grace of God.

There are many things involved with what makes an engine function, but with the manifolds, they receive the gases that are sent into them and distribute them equally to each cylinder. With this act the stage is set for an explosion within the walls of that cylinder, which releases a force to cause something to move. When this is done, the operator of the engine and others are blessed.

As members of the Body of Christ, with each one not being just like another, we are to function like the many different parts of an engine. Each part is important both in the engine and in the body of Christ.

We need the manifold grace of God in our lives for us to function properly. When we function properly, the way God designed us to function, the body will produce all the works of Jesus.

Remember manifolds are used to distribute things into the engine and out of the engine. When we operate and function in the many sides, varieties, and forms of God's grace, we will cause an explosion within the walls of the Body of Christ that will benefit others and us.

Because the manifold of an engine distributes the gas when someone turns a starter key a chain reaction takes place within the electrical system that sets off a spark within the cylinder walls. This causes an explosion that causes the pistons to turn the crankshaft, which turns the transmission causing the wheel to turn. The benefit is that something moves.

With us as engines for the Lord, we are to keep our batteries charged, our tanks full, and use our faith to turn the starter key, so the power of grace can be released to cause an explosion of the things of God causing something to move. I am telling you when grace is ignited, things move. Please note: just as in the engine there are many ingredients in the fuel that support this explosion. There are many ingredients mixed in with this grace, ingredients such as God's Word, and things of the Holy Spirit, love, and forgiveness. So what moves? First, the things of God keep on moving. Then the devil and his spirits move, and mountains move.

There is nothing wrong with the design or blueprint of this Holy Ghost engine—the problem is there are some parts that need a tune-up. There are also parts that need to be restored. Then there are parts that just need to have their fuel tank filled, and yet some just need to crank-up and go.

Bear with the engine illustration. With the engine, no part can operate properly if it is separated from another part. Also, each part is made operative by how another part functions. If we do not operate in love, faith, and grace, it hinders the operation of God's engine—the Body of Christ, the Church.

So, let us make a decision each and every day that we are going to allow the Word of God and the Holy Ghost to do their work in us, for us, and through us. Then we will not frustrate the grace of God from operating in our lives and the lives of others.

> **Great grace to you and through you.**

About the Author

James Rushton has been in the full-time ministry since 1981. After James and his wife graduated from Rhema Bible Training Center, they ministered in the Philippine Islands for twelve years. Since returning, James has ministered throughout the US and in India, Brazil, Kenya, Italy, and Indonesia on healing, the Holy Spirit, God's glory, walking by faith, and living and growing in grace. In October of 2007, James ministered in India, where over 8,000 people received Jesus as their personal Lord and Savior. Thousands more received healing and deliverance.

James has taught Healing School in the local church for over three years, with many people receiving healing of cancer, kidney problems, deliverance, and freedom. He has also taught in four different Bible schools. James has written a syllabus and taught many classes on evangelism, all of which end with the students going out on the streets and door to door.

His bold and compassionate teaching style, under the influence of the Holy Spirit, has set the stage for many to receive healing and be equipped to keep their healing and learn how to minister healing to others.

James is the author of *"Another the Same Kind but Different."* In this book, James shares practical insight into the person of the Holy Spirit and how to get

Him actively involved with your life. The Holy Spirit is our very own coach, and He coaches a winning team.

I would like to thank you for the time you took to read this book. I believe it added the good things of God's grace to your life.

If you have never activated God's grace in your life to become His child, born into the family of God, now would be a good time for you to do so. It is my prayer you have been influenced by the grace and love of God to the point you call on Him to be saved. It is very simple to do. You just use the faith He gave you to confess with your mouth a prayer such as the following:

Prayer

I believe in my heart that Jesus is the Son of God, and I believe He was raised from the dead after paying the price for my being separated from God because of sin.

If you have confessed this belief in your heart, you are a child of God, and you have activated the grace of God to be saved. You are now a part of the Body of the Lord Jesus Christ. Welcome to the family!

Live your life from this day forth by keeping God's grace activated in your life and growing in that grace.

AUTHOR CONTACT INFOMATION

James A. Rushton Ministries
P. O. Box 1663
Brick, NJ 08723-1663
Phone:732-966-3290
E-Mail:rushton787@msn.com
Web Site:www.jrushtonministries.org

CPSIA information can be obtained
at www.ICGtesting.com
Printed in the USA
FFOW02n2047280816
27074FF